ORDINATION

APPROVED *by* GOD
and
SEPARATED *for* SERVICE

HENRY W. WRIGHT

Be in Health™

4178 Crest Highway
Thomaston, Georgia 30286
800-453-5775

www.beinhealth.com

Copyright Notice

Disclaimer

This ministry does not seek to be in conflict with any medical or psychiatric practices nor do we seek to be in conflict with any church and its religious doctrines, beliefs or practices. We are not a part of medicine or psychology, yet we work to make them more effective, rather than working against them. We believe many human problems are fundamentally spiritual with associated physiological and psychological manifestations. This information is intended for your general knowledge only. Information is presented only to give insight into disease, its problems and its possible solutions in the area of disease eradication and/or prevention. It is not a substitute for medical advice or treatment for specific medical conditions or disorders. You should seek prompt medical care for any specific health issues. Treatment modalities around your specific health issues are between you and your physician.

As pastors, ministers and individuals of this ministry, we are not responsible for a person's disease, nor are we responsible for his/her healing. All we can do is share what we see about a problem. We are not professionals; we are not healers. We are only ministers, ministering the Scriptures, and what they say about this subject, along with what the medical and scientific communities have also observed in line with this insight. There is no guarantee that any person will be healed or any disease be prevented. The fruit of   this teaching will come forth out of the relationship between the person and God based on these insights,   given and applied. This ministry is patterned after the following scriptures: 2 Corinthians 5:18-20; 1 Corinthians 12; Ephesians 4; Mark 16:15-20.

Preface

This booklet was developed from a teaching to a live audience and has been kept in a conversational format. It is designed to reach a personal level with the reader rather than present a structured, theological presentation. Many times the reader will feel that Pastor Henry is talking directly to him or her. The frequent use of the pronoun you is meant to penetrate the human heart for conviction, not for accusation. Pastor Henry has been called to the office of pastor, and as such, he takes care of God's flock (whereas one called to the office of teacher does not take care of the sheep).

BUT HE THAT IS GREATEST

AMONG YOU

SHALL BE YOUR SERVANT.

MATTHEW 23:11

This booklet sets forth the guidelines used at Pleasant Valley Church for the ordination of a pastor. This is a transcript of the ordination of a pastor in a closed meeting.

Table of Contents

ORDINATION

OLD TESTAMENT PATTERN

I want to discuss the parameters of this ordination because many of us are aware of traditional, even ungodly order. Very few churches have proper government because men have intruded into the scriptural foundation for leadership. Most churches in America today are ruled by deacons who hire and fire the elders or pastors. This is the most ungodly method of government there is. I know it is done to control ungodly elders or pastors, but they are God's problem.

The Scriptures are filled with information about ordination, and I want to show you the patterns. This message is being recorded to set precedence for how the leadership thinks at Pleasant Valley Church.

The Christian church is not a democracy even though in some churches today, people get to vote on who their pastor will be. That is unscriptural. There is not one scripture to validate a democracy in Christianity, not even one. The government of God is a theocracy.

SERVING FROM THE HEART

I am going to lay this out because we are ordaining a pastor at Pleasant Valley Church. This man has certainly proven himself over the years as a deacon. It is time to kick it up a notch, and it does not make any difference where you have served. The kingdom of God is one kingdom, one Lord, one faith, one baptism, one God and one Father of all. There is no such thing as denominations in the Bible. So however you have served mankind from your heart counts in heaven because it's giving service unto the Lord, not unto men. Examples include service from the heart to the community, such as participation in a Christmas stocking fund and service to the community in the Chamber of Commerce leadership meetings, which extends far beyond the walls of a denomination.

Service also includes that given within the walls of this church, which is a local assembly of a body of believers who gather together as a New Testament fellowship. The Bible tells us about the church of Pergamos, the church of Laodicea, and the church at Ephesus. I am telling you about the church of Thomaston.

SYNAGOGUES

The pattern of the Old Testament church in Jesus' day was that of synagogues in local blocks. There would have been only one church of Thomaston. I did not find the word "synagogues" in my study, so that was "man breaking down his city." Usually the synagogue was eight to twelve families. With reference to this local block area back in the Old Testament, they were part of Israel, and the government and the church were one. There was no separation of church and state, so everyone who lived in the community was Jewish. They were God's people. Every block area had a little local synagogue where everyone attended. The synagogue served that block. Then, as was their tradition, once a year they came to a big conclave during the Passover.

The kingdom of God is a theocracy, and we all serve under the head bishop, Jesus Christ. He is called the bishop of the church.

For ye were as sheep going astray; but are now returned unto the Shepherd and Bishop of your souls. 1 Peter 2:25

Jesus serves the Father; then the Holy Spirit executes that government in the earth through humans. Humans should not interfere with God, but God has the right to interfere with humans.

In Exodus during the beginning of the Old Testament church, Moses, as the first pastor, was beginning to have a church that was too large. He had over 3 million, and he was trying to do it all himself. Moses' father-in-law came to him and rebuked him. He told him he was in sin, ungodly, and he was doing it wrong. In fact, he said, "You are not doing a very good job by yourself."

> ¹⁴And when Moses' father-in-law saw all that he did to the people, he said, What is this thing that thou doest to the people? why sittest thou thyself alone, and all the people stand by thee from morning unto even?
> ¹⁵And Moses said unto his father-in-law, Because the people come unto me to enquire of God.
> ¹⁶When they have a matter, they come unto me; and I judge between one and another, and I do make them know the statutes of God, and his laws.
> Exodus 18:14-16

HOW GOD THINKS

The first tenet of leadership is teaching the people how God thinks. How do we know how God thinks? We know how He thinks because of what He said. How do we know what He said? We read the Scriptures. Holy men, moved by the Holy Spirit, wrote as the Spirit of God gave them inspiration.

For the prophecy came not in old time by the will of man: but holy men of God spake as they were moved by the Holy Ghost.   2 Peter 1:21

All scripture is given by inspiration of God...
                    2 Timothy 3:16

In the case of Moses, however, his knowledge was given directly to him, not by the Holy Spirit, but by the Lord Himself, in His preincarnate state as the God of Israel.

Let's go to Exodus.

¹⁷And Moses' father-in-law said unto him, The thing that thou doest is not good.
¹⁸Thou wilt surely wear away, both thou, and this people that *is* with thee: for this thing *is* too heavy for thee; thou art not able to perform it thyself alone.
¹⁹Hearken now unto my voice, I will give thee counsel, and God shall be with thee.   Exodus 18:17-19

Jethro became a prophet. He did not even understand that he had a spirit of prophecy on him.

¹⁹ ...Be thou for the people to Godward, that thou mayest bring the causes unto God:
²⁰And thou shalt teach them ordinances and laws, and shalt shew them the way wherein they must walk, and the work that they must do.
                    Exodus 18:19-20

Who are "they?" God's people!

> Moreover thou shalt provide out of all the people able men, such as fear God, men of truth, hating covetousness; and place *such* over them, *to be* rulers of thousands, *and* rulers of hundreds, rulers of fifties, and rulers of tens: Exodus 18:21

Who does "them" refer to? God's people!

SOME QUALIFICATIONS

- Able men such as fear God
- Men of truth
- Hating covetousness

This means you cannot be bribed or bought. Some can be bribed, bought and tempted with fame and gain.

> And let them judge the people at all seasons: and it shall be, *that* every great matter they shall bring unto thee, but every small matter they shall judge: so shall it be easier for thyself, and they shall bear *the burden* with thee.   Exodus 18:22

NEW TESTAMENT PATTERN

> [7]But unto every one of us is given grace according to the measure of the gift of Christ.
> [8]Wherefore he saith, When he ascended up on high, he led captivity captive, and gave gifts unto men.
> Ephesians 4:7-8

Who is that scripture talking about? Jesus!

It also says "and gave gifts unto men."

> [9](Now that he ascended, what is it but that he also descended first into the lower parts of the earth?
> [10]He that descended is the same also that ascended up far above all heavens, that he might fill all things.)
> Ephesians 4:9-10

Colossians says,

> And he is the head of the body, the church: who is the beginning, the firstborn from the dead; that in all things he might have the preeminence.
> Colossians 1:18

The "head of the body" is referring to Jesus. The body of Christ is made up of people, the church.

We very clearly understand that Jesus is the head of the church, and He is the one in Ephesians 4:8 who is giving gifts unto men. These gifts are not the nine gifts of the Holy Spirit as it has been sometimes taught.

FIVEFOLD MINISTRY

Ephesians tells you what, or rather who, the gifts are. He gave these gifts out of the people.

> And he gave some, apostles; and some, prophets; and some, evangelists; and some, pastors and teachers;   Ephesians 4:11

This is referred to as the fivefold ministry. These are your elders in Christianity.

YOU CANNOT BE AN ELDER IN THE LOCAL ASSEMBLY IF YOU ARE NOT ONE OF THESE FIVE CLASSIFICATIONS.

I have seen it misused so many ways. In our ordination today, the word "elder" is a title. These five titles are positions.

There is a difference between a title and a position. All five of these are elders, but the position indicates what type of gift they are from the Lord. I am not promoting myself, but I promise you, I am a gift from Jesus to mankind. Every believer is a gift from God, as the priesthood of believers. God has set the fivefold ministry over that priesthood of believers.

> Now ye are the body of Christ, and members in particular. 1 Corinthians 12:27

In this case the word "God" means the Father. If you go back to Colossians, it is obviously referring to God the Father, His ordination, and His work of service through Jesus.

> For by him were all things created, that are in heaven, and that are in earth, visible and invisible, whether they be thrones, or dominions, or principalities, or powers: all things were created by him, and for him: Colossians 1:16

A large percentage of Christianity has removed most of verse 28. Many churches do not incorporate all of verse 28 in their governmental structure; therefore they are not truly following Christ because if God the Father and the Lord Jesus as the head Bishop placed these things in the church, then what kind of anarchy removes it?

> And God hath set some in the church, first apostles, secondarily prophets, thirdly teachers, after that miracles, then gifts of healings, helps, governments, diversities of tongues.
> 1 Corinthians 12:28

DISPENSATION FOR TODAY

It is no wonder we have problems in our churches and families. We all say, "I love you, Jesus," yet we are in absolute rebellion to His government and the theocracy of His intent. If I said this in many

9

churches I know it would not be very popular, but I did not write the Bible. I am not going to change it. In most churches today, there is no apostle present because they say apostles passed away 2,000 years ago. They say there are no prophets today because they were in the Old Testament. Ephesians 4:11 and 1 Corinthians 12:28 are not Old Testament scriptures.

By the way, the author is Paul who was not even one of the twelve. He is the apostle of the New Testament dispensation, and he is establishing it. The New Testament church that Paul spoke of and established in power is in the same dispensation of time that we are in now, so the rules are the same.

APOSTASY – HERESY

I want to expose the ecclesiastical apostasy of churches and their government. There are denominations in America that require their ministers to have degrees from a school of theology in order for them to understand the Bible. This decision was established at their annual conferences. The Roman Catholic Church also did that hundreds of years ago when they put the Word into the hands of a few (the priests) and then changed the language into Latin so that no one else understood it. They then placed the Bible on the forbidden book list. We are very close to that again. We are not there yet, but it could happen quickly. It could be taught that only a few people are allowed to hear God and understand truth. That is absolute heresy!

APPOINTED BY GOD

As we are about to appoint and ordain you by our leadership in this local assembly, under the oversight of the Lord Jesus Christ and the Father, I want to make sure that you, as a newly ordained pastor, are not burdened by the irrelevance of apostate leaders who will disagree with your positioning. They will look at you and say you do not meet their criteria of who should be a pastor. They are not the ones that appointed you; I am not appointing you either.

In this meeting of those who are your peers, we are looking at you and seeing the gifts that are already in your lives. We did not create them. We did not train you in them. They have been developed from within you, just the same as in Exodus 18:21, 25 when Jethro told Moses to look in the midst of the people and find those who were already known to be gifts to the people. Did they go through the "captain of ten" school? Did they go through the "captain of fifty" school? Did they go through the "captain of one hundred" school? Did they go through the "captain of one thousand" school? No, they were given 10, 50, 100 or 1,000 that very first day and told to take care of business. If you have a problem, get your instruction from Moses because he also heard God for you. This narrows down the concern in a hurry.

ELDERS

Let's look at the New Testament example of how elders were chosen. The elders of the New Testament church were not chosen from the elders of the Old Testament church. The Lord did not take one elder of the Old Testament church and make him an elder of the New Testament church, except for Paul, who was a student of the law. Philippians 3:5-6 tells us that Paul, as touching the law, was perfect. He was an elder in the Old Testament church, but he resisted the powers until the Lord had an encounter with him. Then he quickly saw the picture and had a conversion, but he was the only elder that was chosen. The rest were rejected.

Let's look at the New Testament standard in Acts 6:2.

> ²Then the twelve called the multitude of the disciples *unto them*, and said, It is not reason that we should leave the word of God, and serve tables.
> ³Wherefore, brethren, look ye out among you seven men of honest report, full of the Holy Ghost and wisdom...   Acts 6:2-3

MORE QUALIFICATIONS

- Honest report
- Full of the Holy Ghost and wisdom

This is a new condition. Not all the elders in our churches are full of the Holy Ghost. In fact, some deny the infilling of the Holy Ghost. They say they are born again by the Spirit of God, but they are not full of the Holy Ghost. If they were full of the Holy Ghost, the Holy Ghost would get something done through them. They spend most of their time telling you why the Holy Ghost cannot function today; however, I want to find ways that reflect that He is busy on this planet. I want to give the Holy Ghost plenty to do so He does not get bored. Let Him loose!

Wisdom means this to me: The distance between your brain and your tongue is not zero. Knowledge is one thing, but knowledge without wisdom is like a jewel in the nose of a pig.

As a jewel of gold in a swine's snout, *so is* **a fair woman which is without discretion.**   Proverbs 11:22

The letter of the law killeth, but the Spirit giveth life.

Who also hath made us able ministers of the new testament; not of the letter, but of the spirit: for the letter killeth, but the spirit giveth life.
2 Corinthians 3:6

13

So we are not interested in using the Word as a weapon. We are interested in using the Word as a crowbar to pry people loose and send them forth in proper directions.

Let's continue to read.

> ³...whom we may appoint over this business
> ⁴But we will give ourselves continually to prayer, and to the ministry of the word.
> ⁵And the saying pleased the whole multitude: and they chose Stephen, a man full of faith and of the Holy Ghost, and Philip, and Prochorus, and Nicanor, and Timon, and Parmenas, and Nicolas a proselyte of Antioch:
> ⁶Whom they set before the apostles: and when they had prayed, they laid *their* hands on them.
>
> Acts 6:3-6

When they had prayed, they laid their hands on them. That is what we are going to do here today.

GIFTINGS MAKE ROOM

They took people out of the flock who already were operating in their gifting, which was recognized. That is why the Bible says a man's gift shall make room for him.

> A man's gift maketh room for him, and bringeth him before great men.　　Proverbs 18:16

Concerning the gifts of the Holy Spirit, Corinthians says, "dividing severally as he will."

> But all these worketh that one and the selfsame
> Spirit, dividing to every man severally as he will.
> 1 Corinthians 12:11

He is watching. He knows us. He is trying the reins of our hearts. He leads us. He promotes us. He stirs us. He gives us desires. He equips us. Then in the flow of things, the elders will notice it.

We will say, "Hey! Where did he come from? Look what they are doing!"

Now there is a counterfeit of men who will come and appear to be led by the Spirit of God, but who have agendas of pride and fame. That is why the Bible says not to appoint or promote a novice before his time because he will be puffed up in pride.

> Not a novice, lest being lifted up with pride he
> fall into the condemnation of the devil.   1 Timothy 3:6

SERVICE

There must be a measure of time so that we can observe a person's maturity and growth. In the New Testament, they recognized an individual's giftings. They went to him and said, "Would you like to serve?"

So we came to you and asked, "Would you like to serve at a different level?" We noticed you. You have been here for a while. We have watched you grow. We think you have a heart for the people and

15

the town. We would like you to serve with us in honor, and we are going to include you in the government of His kingdom. So we are all practicing to be kings and priests in the millennium. This is a good time to practice, right here in this church. You are going to practice for an age and a time that is not here yet, but this is where you practice to see what kind of stuff you are made of.

I have always been challenged by the Old Testament. Elijah was a great prophet. Now they did not create a school of prophets to train them how to be a prophet. God decides who the prophets are. You cannot train someone to be a prophet.

I don't think you can train a man to be a pastor either. You cannot be a pastor unless you have a pastor's heart. Most seminaries of learning do not teach you how to have a pastor's heart or teach you how to rule a sheepfold. Many pastors should not be pastors, because they don't like the sheep. You cannot teach a man how to really be a teacher unless he has a revelation of teaching in his own heart. Otherwise he is just a mouthpiece, and there is no anointing.

You cannot teach a man how to be an evangelist. He's going to have to have something in his heart that burns. You cannot teach a man how to be an apostle. He is going to have to learn how to guard doctrine and guard the flock. All these things come sovereignly from within each individual. When I see the work of the Holy Spirit in a person's life, I help him grow into his office because the fivefold ministry is an office. The word "elder" is just a title. The office tells me who you are.

CHOSEN TO SERVE

In the church you already see a work of the Holy Spirit. There were officers of the corporate church operating in their office as a member of the fivefold ministry such as Barnabas, Simeon, Lucius and Manaen.

> Now there were in the church that was at Antioch certain prophets and teachers; as Barnabas, and Simeon that was called Niger, and Lucius of Cyrene, and Manaen, which had been brought up with Herod the tetrarch, and Saul.   Acts 13:1

Then the Holy Ghost said, "Now." Did they hear the voice of the Holy Ghost? Could they hear the voice of the Holy Ghost audibly in the room? What is meant by "the Holy Ghost said?" It means that He caused thoughts to form that bore witness in all of the men that are listed in verse one.

> As they ministered to the Lord, and fasted, the Holy Ghost said, Separate me Barnabas and Saul for the work whereunto I have called them.   Acts 13:2

They all heard the Holy Spirit and came to a consensus. In our decision as the ruling elders and elders of this local fellowship, the Holy Ghost bore witness and said: Choose this one.

HEARTS TRIED

We have had other pastors in this church, but we did not ordain them. We did not bring them into a room like this because the Holy Ghost did not tell me to do it that way with them.

So in Acts 13:2, it says, "And the Holy Ghost said." Over the years, I have not been quick to ordain anyone. Now the word "ordain" is man's term. Men like to hear, "I have been ordained." No, it is correct to say: *You have been separated from the flock for service.*

In fact, in the certificate that we are going to give you today, to make sure that we are clear on this, in the certificate that we are going to give you today it reads:

> "We, the undersigned, hereby certify that upon the recommendation and request of Pleasant Valley Church Inc. of Thomaston, GA, which had full and sufficient opportunity for judging his gifts, and after satisfactory examination by us in regard to his Christian experience, call to the ministry and review the Bible doctrine, (name of person being ordained), a servant of Jesus Christ, called to be a pastor,

separated and ordained unto the gospel of God..."

Paul, a servant of Jesus Christ, called *to be* an apostle, separated unto the gospel of God,
Romans 1:1

We have a statement right out of Romans 1:1. "Unto the Gospel of God by authority and order of Pleasant Valley Church Inc. of Thomaston, Georgia, Ordaining Council," and we will sign that when we are done.

Paul referred to himself in Romans 1:1 as "a servant of Jesus Christ, called to be an apostle."

That was his office. There are five offices. We are not ordaining you as an apostle, a prophet, a teacher, or an evangelist, but as a pastor. It does not mean that one day you couldn't move through the fivefold ministry and become something else, but you must be faithful in the first. I am moving through the stages too, but you must be faithful in the first. This is a process.

SEPARATED BY THE HOLY GHOST

Paul referred to himself as a servant of Jesus Christ called to be an apostle, separated...

We added the word "ordained" to "and ordained unto the gospel of God."

19

So out of the flock, the Holy Spirit is drawing you, separating you for service, to serve the flock. They ministered to the Lord and fasted, and the Holy Spirit said in Acts 13:2, "Separate me Barnabas and Saul for the work whereunto I have called them." (See scripture above.)

So who called Barnabas and Saul for the work of the ministry? The Holy Ghost called them.

So also the Holy Ghost chose you. Men did not choose you. I am not choosing you. I promise you if we did not have the witness of the Holy Spirit, you would not be in this room. So, the Holy Ghost is here. We have a witness.

When they had fasted and prayed, they laid their hands on them. I like what it says next: "and sent them away."

And when they had fasted and prayed, and laid *their* hands on them, they sent *them* away.   Acts 13:3

Do you know what that means? Get on with it! Now, in both cases in Acts 6 and Acts 13, from both elders and deacons, the members of the fivefold ministry that were in place at that time laid their hands on them, prayed and released them to be separated for service. That is all we are going to do today. That's all they did. I don't know why anyone would do more than this, unless they needed to for their own reasons.

Anyone who would question your selection for service, not at Pleasant Valley Church, but in the corporate body of Christ globally needs to recognize that there is only one church. If people ever question your ordination because you did not go through seminary, I challenge them to find the word "doctor" in scripture. They even tried to call Jesus doctor. He said, "Do not call me doctor. Do not call me Rabbi."

> And Jesus said unto him, Why callest thou me good? *there is* none good but one, *that is*, God.
> Mark 10:18

He would not even accept the title of teacher or doctor of the law, but they perceived He knew the law better than they did. If that is the attitude of the Bishop of the church, why should we have a different attitude? In fact, you don't need to be approved of men; you need to be approved of God. If I can't find something in scripture, I am not going to do it. Acts 2:22 tells us how we know we are approved of God. If I cannot find it in scripture, I am not going to do it. The book of Acts says, "The man, Jesus Christ of Nazareth, had to be approved by God Himself and separated unto service."

> Ye men of Israel, hear these words; Jesus of Nazareth, a man approved of God among you by miracles and wonders and signs, which God did by him in the midst of you, as ye yourselves also know:
> Acts 2:22

MORE QUALIFICATIONS

- Approved by God

There is your ordination.

I promise you, there are not many people being ordained in America and around the world today, for whom miracles and wonders and signs are even a condition. In fact, they removed the conditions of approval, because if you cannot do miracles and wonders and signs, there is no proof that you are called of God. There is no proof, because you have a gospel that is polluted by dead works. Do you see it? Jesus Himself needed to be approved of God. This is powerful, isn't it?

In Acts, it says, "and they sent them away." So they were being sent forth by whom? By the Holy Ghost.

Continuing,

> ³And when they had fasted and prayed, and laid *their* hands on them, they sent *them* away.
> ⁴So they, being sent forth by the Holy Ghost, departed unto Seleucia; and from thence they sailed to Cyprus.
> ⁵And when they were at Salamis, they preached the word of God in the synagogues of the Jews: and they had also John to *their* minister.   Acts 13:3-5

(We have been sent forth into South Africa, England and Singapore.)

When they preached the Word, they preached the Word in churches that did not ordain them because they were not part of the religious system. These were men who were chosen by the Holy Ghost, not by men. The rulers of the synagogue were chosen by men. We can't teach that too loudly. They preached the Word of God in the Old Testament church, the synagogues of the Jews, and they also had John as their minister.

OFFICE OF A BISHOP

Here you see the movement. You all know this verse in 1 Timothy 3:1 because you read it before at the time you were practicing to become deacons. This *is* a true saying,

If a man desire the office of a bishop, he desireth a good work.   1 Timothy 3:1

Let's talk about who a bishop is. A bishop is an elder. "Bishop" is a title. "Elder" is a title, but it tells you nothing about the office. So a bishop is one who has an office, and there are only five offices listed in scripture other than deacon: apostle, prophet, evangelist, pastor and teacher. So anyone that is an apostle, a prophet, an evangelist, a pastor or a teacher is a bishop. Certain people, groups and denominations make a big thing out of the title of bishop. "I am bishop over all these elders." No you are not; you are a bishop over bishops.

ORDER OF GOVERNMENT

Everyone is an equal bishop, but there is an order of the government of bishops. No one is greater than the other, but there is a distinction of the office. They have apostles, prophets, evangelists, pastors and teachers in that order. That is the order of the government of God. So a teacher should be in subjection to an apostle, a pastor should be in subjection to an apostle, an evangelist should be in subjection to an apostle, and a prophet should be in subjection to a true apostle.

In that subjection to the apostle, they are equal, but there is an order of responsibility. "Order of responsibility" is a key phrase. The pastors at Pleasant Valley Church are all bishops. Technically and scripturally, you are a bishop as of today, operating in the office of pastor. When I finish this, it sets in order what is happening here forever. Not only for you, but also for anyone else that would serve under the ecclesiastical positioning order in this local church.

Timothy says that a man who desires the office of a bishop desires a good work. So bishops work, and your greatness is your service.

But he that is greatest among you shall be your servant.   Matthew 23:11

Jesus' greatness was His service.

MORE QUALIFICATIONS

- Husband of one wife

A bishop then must be blameless, the husband of one wife, vigilant, sober, of good behavior, given to hospitality, apt to teach; 1 Timothy 3:2

MANY ERRONEOUSLY USE THIS SCRIPTURE TO TRY TO PROVE THAT THE MAN WHO HAS BEEN DIVORCED AND REMARRIED DOES NOT QUALIFY.

In both the context of paganism and historical Jewish understanding, a man could have more than one wife. In the movement from the Old Testament to the New Testament, it was strongly taught and believed, as a work of the Holy Spirit, that one wife at a time was enough. That is my position. It would be difficult for me to be a Pastor here and have two wives.

Donna has all my time, and she knows that she is not going to share me with anyone. It would not be good for the church if I were torn between two women. I want that position stated in this teaching because it is a big argument. I have one wife.

MORE QUALIFICATIONS

- Given to hospitality
- Vigilant
- Sober
- Of good behavior
- Given to hospitality
- Able to teach

"Given to hospitality." We have observed your hospitality.

"Able to teach." Let's look at 2 Timothy.

> ²⁴And the servant of the Lord must not strive; but be gentle unto all *men*, apt to teach, patient,
> ²⁵In meekness instructing those that oppose themselves; if God peradventure will give them repentance to the acknowledging of the truth;
> ²⁶And *that* they may recover themselves out of the snare of the devil, who are taken captive by him at his will. 2 Timothy 2:24-26

- Not given to wine

Timothy says,

> Not given to wine... 1 Timothy 3:3

"Not given to wine" means you do not have your mouth at the spigot; you don't have to have alcohol in your blood stream. Let me discuss something about wine. The Bible is very clear that you should not be a winebibber.

> **Be not among winebibbers; among riotous eaters of flesh:** Proverbs 23:20

In Proverbs, Lemuel's mother tells him that the reason a man, a leader, should not get drunk is because he will pervert the justice of the people. Other scriptures indicate that you should not be given to wine in excess.

> **⁴*It is* not for kings, O Lemuel, *it is* not for kings to drink wine; nor for princes strong drink:**
> **⁵Lest they drink, and forget the law, and pervert the judgment of any of the afflicted.** Proverbs 31:4-5

I do not babysit people's lives. Some say that you can drink wine in France, but you cannot drink it here. Because the water is not good over there, they drink wine. I'll say this officially at this level: I do not like to see people coming into a church sitting with alcohol on their breath.

Paul is very clear that you can't take your liberty as a license if it offends your brother. Your action may not be sin, but offending your brother is sin.

It is good neither to eat flesh, nor to drink wine,
nor *any thing* whereby thy brother stumbleth, or is
offended, or is made weak.   Romans 14:21

When you are in settings where someone is having a glass of wine, you can't make him unclean. You can't establish yourself as more righteous than he is over this one issue.

The Lord has taken the position that your freedom should not offend your brother who is weak in the faith.

So I would say this to you officially: If you decide to have a glass of wine with your food or with your friends in a private setting, it would not be offensive. I'll not call that sin in your life as long as it is not abusive and excessive. I'll not police you, but if there seems to be a predisposition to a lot of wine, there may be an addiction. There may be a problem that would not be proper for a leader to have. I'll probably get in trouble with a lot of people for even giving you your own lives at this level, but I am not going to babysit you. Everything must be done decently, without reproach, and we should conduct ourselves in a godly way.

DO NOT BE
A STUMBLING BLOCK
TO OTHERS
IN A PUBLIC SETTING.

Moderation is a big teaching. Also we can get into the definition of wine, whether it was fermented or not fermented. We can go all over the place with this, but I am not going there because I have more important things to do than to be your conscience. You know what I am talking about, so I am not going to get magnifying glasses and look at the speck in everyone's eye. That's not what we are called to. We are called to govern at levels that bring moderation and direction. However, if a person believes that having a glass of wine is sin, to him it is sin.

We could go over to Romans 14. If you think that eating meat is sin, then to you eating it is a sin. If I eat meat it is not sin to me, but if you think you should be a vegetarian and you eat meat, it is sin to you. The issue is tied to your own conscience. Your conscience may be free, or your conscience may not be free, but the Lord wants you to follow the dictates of your own conscience, because otherwise what are you going to follow? Some other man's conscience? So I would say in this conversation, I want men to follow their own conscience, and if their conscience is evil, we will know it soon enough.

The letter of the law kills, horribly. If I am eating meat, you have no right to say anything to me, because I eat unto the Lord.

I suggest that all of you read Romans 14 at some point, and get this clearly in your mind, so you are not caught by those who want to argue over meat and drink.

> **14I know, and am persuaded by the Lord Jesus, that *there is* nothing unclean of itself: but to him that esteemeth any thing to be unclean, to him *it is* unclean.**
> **15But if thy brother be grieved with *thy* meat, now walkest thou not charitably. Destroy not him with thy meat, for whom Christ died.** Romans 14:14-15

I will tell you this.

> **For the kingdom of God is not meat and drink; but righteousness, and peace, and joy in the Holy Ghost.** Romans 14:17

On the other hand, this conversation is not a license to go out and do anything you want. It is simply a balanced statement that you can follow in your heart. If I suddenly appear at your house when you are having dinner and a glass of wine, you do not have to turn red and hide it.

You can decline if you feel it is an addictive reality. If it is a custom or a culture of serving wine at dinner and you are invited, yet you sense it is going to continue until they kill 14 gallons of it, then you can decline because it would be "in excess" instead of "in moderation." You can't decline based on counting wine as sin and you being righteous for not having any. You can decline because that obviously would be lack of moderation, wine to excess, and it would then be sin.

Not given to wine, no striker, not greedy of filthy lucre; but patient, not a brawler, not covetous;
1 Timothy 3:3

- No striker

"No striker." In *Strong's*, that means a smiter; pugnacious (quarrelsome).

- Not greedy of filthy lucre

Not greedy of filthy lucre! That means you can't be bribed; you are not doing it for money.

- Patient
- Not a brawler

"Patient, not a brawler." This means you can't come in here and start knocking people to the side of the wall because you do not agree with them. In *Strong's* it is defined as a peaceable person.

- Not covetous

"Not covetous" means you are happy with the things you have.

- Ruleth well his own house

Timothy says,

⁴One that ruleth well his own house, having his children in subjection with all gravity;
⁵(For if a man know not how to rule his own house, how shall he take care of the church of God?)
1 Timothy 3:4-5

We have been tested in this one as to putting our kids out on the street. We have to give them the option to leave or stay, and we have done it. We have lived it, because we cannot judge our own home. I think the record stands for itself.

[Pastor Donna] The scripture he just read used to condemn me because I thought that if we were good parents, then our children would turn out perfect. Well, I later found out through Henry talking to me, that the scripture does not mean what I thought.

What God's Word says is that we could not have this corruption in our home, so they had to choose. We took this position: You cannot act up and be corrupt in our home without having to leave. That was very hard because as a mom, I certainly did not want them to ever be corrupt. Even more, I certainly did not want them to be corrupted on the street. God has honored our heart.

So we have ruled with righteousness instead of enabling. I am sure the days are coming when we will reap the benefits of that, and I know that God is in this. It cleansed my heart, so I did not feel guilty.

EXAMPLE OF ENABLING FATHER

[Pastor Henry] Samuel grew up under Eli as the head priest of the kingdom, but Eli had two sons who came in and corrupted the temple. Yet Eli did nothing; he did not even rebuke his sons. He did not even say, "You are corrupt boys, and you have to stay away from the house of God." He allowed them to come into the temple with prostitutes and do all kinds of stuff, and he was judged for that. In fact, he fell over backwards and broke his neck and died. It is very clear that God was displeased by the fact that he would not judge his own house. Now, Samuel came and took Eli's place as a prophet. Samuel did not know he was coming as his replacement, but God knew.

What will you do when you are faced with situations?

ARE YOU GOING TO RULE
IN FAVOR OF YOUR CHILDREN
IN THEIR UNGODLINESS
BECAUSE YOU LOVE THEM?
- OR -
ARE YOU GOING TO RULE
ACCORDING TO
WHAT GOD'S WORD SAYS?

This is a big issue. We don't want believers to feel condemned because their children are ungodly. If your children are not perfect, especially since you live in a fishbowl and people say, "Ahhh. Did you know about...?" You can't even let that touch you. You can't let that bother you because that is their evil. That is their sin. You are not evil, and your children don't have to be perfect.

WILL YOU
REPRESENT GOD TO YOUR FAMILY
PROPERLY?

This instruction is to release you from that "fishbowl mentality" because it is not true.

Rule your home with righteousness, not with enabling. Verses 6-7 say,

>⁶Not a novice, lest being lifted up with pride he fall into the condemnation of the devil.
>⁷Moreover he must have a good report of them which are without; lest he fall into reproach and the snare of the devil.   1 Timothy 3:6-7

MORE QUALIFICATIONS

- Not a novice

- Of good report

- Grave

- Not double-tongued

> Likewise *must* the deacons *be* grave, not double-tongued, not given to much wine, not greedy of filthy lucre;   1 Timothy 3:8

"Not double-tongued." In other words, we can take you to the bank when you talk. You cannot say one thing to one person and something else to another, because that means you are double-minded and unstable. One thing is for sure; with me you pretty much know where I stand with everyone. I don't have an agenda. What you see is what you get all the time, and that is good. You may not like it at times, but I do not have an evil agenda behind it. I do not have an evil heart towards people. So the deacons must be grave, not double-tongued.

- Not given to much wine

It does not say they cannot have wine. It says, "not given to much wine." We have talked about this before.

- Not greedy of filthy lucre

"Not greedy of filthy lucre" refers to money and our greed for money.

>⁹Holding the mystery of the faith in a pure conscience.
>¹⁰And let these also first be proved; then let them use the office of a deacon, being *found* blameless.
>¹¹Even so *must their* wives *be* grave, not slanderers, sober, faithful in all things.
>¹²Let the deacons be the husbands of one wife, ruling their children and their own houses well.
>¹³For they that have used the office of a deacon well purchase to themselves a good degree, and great boldness in the faith which is in Christ Jesus.
>
>1 Timothy 3:9-13

- Holding the mystery of the faith in pure conscience

There is your degree. So if you are asked, "Do you have a degree?" say, "Yes, I have a good degree — a good degree and great boldness in the faith which is in Christ Jesus." In this fellowship, as we move along, we may appoint some deacons to serve the bishops. There's a lot here that I am thinking of because deacons are part of the government. It is a good training ground to become a member of the fivefold ministry. We now have four generations going to this church, and the older we get, the more we want to raise up the younger ones. We do not want to end up with a church of just old people who die. We want to begin training every level of every generation to be a governing level within themselves and able to move through this.

I want to give an exhortation, and then we are going to lay hands on you and pray and then release you. We are going to send you out. I am going to send you away!

I want to read the entire chapter of 1 Timothy 4 as an exhortation. This is to all of us because it speaks for itself.

EXHORTATION

¹Now the Spirit speaketh expressly, that in the latter times some shall depart from the faith, giving heed to seducing spirits, and doctrines of devils;

²Speaking lies in hypocrisy; having their conscience seared with a hot iron;

³Forbidding to marry, and *commanding* to abstain from meats, which God hath created to be received with thanksgiving of them which believe and know the truth.

⁴For every creature of God *is* good, and nothing to be refused, if it be received with thanksgiving:

1 Timothy 4:1-4

This is a dietary issue. You are going to bump into people who are coming out of churches and movements which teach that the things forbidden under the law are forbidden today. First Timothy 4:4 says just the opposite.

[Pastor Donna] They are going to question you and say, "Well, is it really considered food? Has it ever been considered food?"

[Pastor Henry] It is talking about food. It is talking about meats.

[Pastor Donna] Some say that shellfish were never considered to be a food.

[Pastor Henry] But it says *every* creature. The chapter that goes along with this is Romans 14. That way, we have the Word instead of the debate. They do not have the Word, just the debate.

> ¹Him that is weak in the faith receive ye, *but* not to doubtful disputations.
> ²For one believeth that he may eat all things: another, who is weak, eateth herbs.
> ³Let not him that eateth despise him that eateth not; and let not him which eateth not judge him that eateth: for God hath received him.
> ⁴Who art thou that judgest another man's servant? to his own master he standeth or falleth. Yea, he shall be holden up: for God is able to make him stand.
> Romans 14:1-4

Let's read more scripture.

> ⁴For every creature of God *is* good, and nothing to be refused, if it be received with thanksgiving:
> ⁵For it is sanctified by the word of God and prayer.   1 Timothy 4:4-5

Timothy says,

> If thou put the brethren in remembrance of these things, thou shalt be a good minister of Jesus Christ, nourished up in the words of faith and of good doctrine, whereunto thou hast attained.   1 Timothy 4:6

MORE QUALIFICATIONS

- Refuse profane and old wives' fables
- Exercise thyself unto godliness
- Trust in the living God

⁷But refuse profane and old wives' fables, and exercise thyself rather unto godliness.

⁸For bodily exercise profiteth little: but godliness is profitable unto all things, having promise of the life that now is, and of that which is to come.

⁹This is a faithful saying and worthy of all acceptation.

¹⁰For therefore we both labor and suffer reproach, because we trust in the living God, who is the Savior of all men, specially of those that believe.

1 Timothy 4:7-10

Do you know what kind of reproach we are getting here in this town simply because we trust totally in the living God, and they think maybe that is evil? God knows! Who is the Savior of all men, especially of those that believe? Not all men believe, but the Lord is the Savior of all those that believe. So being ministers, we bring people into believing. I am not talking about being born again; I am talking about believing the truth.

- Let no man despise thy youth

Timothy says,

> [11]These things command and teach.
> [12]Let no man despise thy youth; but be thou an example of the believers, in word, in conversation, in charity, in spirit, in faith, in purity.
> 1 Timothy 4:11-12

What this really says is that you do not have to be old to represent God in the context of serving. We always hear that we should "Let no man despise thy youth." It has nothing to do with youth. It has to do with the Word of God coming through anyone, no matter what their age is.

- Be an example in word
- Be an example in conversation
- Be an example in charity
- Be an example in spirit
- Be an example in faith
- Be an example in purity

What comes out of our mouth should be truth, in conversation, in charity, in spirit, in faith, in purity.

Continuing,

> [13]Till I come, give attendance to reading, to exhortation, to doctrine.
> [14]Neglect not the gift that is in thee, which was given thee by prophecy, with the laying on of the hands of the presbytery.
> 1 Timothy 4:13-14

These four scriptures are about ordination and the laying on of hands by the presbytery. The bishops are the presbytery or the elders. The elders are members of the fivefold ministry.

Continuing,

15Meditate upon these things; give thyself wholly to them; that thy profiting may appear to all.
16Take heed unto thyself, and unto the doctrine; continue in them: for in doing this thou shalt both save thyself, and them that hear thee.

1 Timothy 4:15-16

My, what a powerful conclusion!

"That you may save all that hear thee" is addressed to the leaders. Not many leaders are being exhorted these days also to continue to save themselves.

That is my little mini-teaching on government, on what we are doing, on why we are doing it, and on how we are doing it. This is the foundation for any questions at this level. Then we are going to follow our hearts as the presbytery of Pleasant Valley Church, which is a local body of believers and a member of the corporate body of Christ. We are going to follow the dictates of the Holy Spirit in our hearts concerning you.

SENDING FORTH

We are going to come over to you, and we are going to stand around you and lay hands on you. We are going to pray and release the Holy Spirit to go with you. He is already in you, but in the figurative understanding, you go out in the power of the Holy Spirit to accomplish what He has placed, and will continue to place, in your hearts to take care of God's flock.

We are going to pray with this husband and wife, and lay hands on them. Just take your peace and join hands. Join hands.

PRAYER

Father God in heaven, we come to You in the name of the Lord Jesus Christ. You, as a work of the Holy Spirit, have placed within our hearts a call for them (husband and wife), and we choose them. We look into their hearts, and we ask You to separate them to Your purposes. From within the flock they came, and from within the flock they will serve. We recognize their giftings of hospitality, and doctrine, and patience, and their heart and care for people. We recognize their care for people that are not really lovely sometimes, and even unlovely sometimes.

Father, we, according to Scripture, lay our hands on them this day, and we bless them. We come into agreement with You, Father, we come into agreement with You, Lord Jesus, and we come into agreement with You, Holy Spirit, that You have chosen this couple for service and for the gospel of our God to be servants, not only of Jesus Christ, but of the Father. Father, we ask that You stretch forth Your mighty hand right now in the name of the Lord Jesus Christ and place Your giftings deep within them to serve You. Cover them, lead them, grow them, anoint them to take care of who You love, God, and that is Your people.

Let Your love come, Father, in compassion. Give them a hunger for Your Word. Give them a hunger for Your people. Give them a hunger for the power of

43

God to break and destroy the works of the devil. I release the Spirit of God to break hell, to confront hell and to defeat hell for Your purposes. Father, let it be accomplished this day.

They are elected, as they are selected from the foundation of the world. We now appoint him, release him, and send him forth in the office of pastor according to the Scriptures. In the name of the Lord Jesus Christ I pray this.

Amen.